CENGAGE Learning

Novels for Students, Volume 36

Project Editor: Sara Constantakis Rights Acquisition and Management: Leitha Etheridge-Sims, Jackie Jones, Tim Sisler Composition: Evi Abou-El-Seoud Manufacturing: Rhonda Dover

Imaging: John Watkins

Product Design: Pamela A. E. Galbreath, Jennifer Wahi Content Conversion: Katrina Coach Product Manager: Meggin Condino © 2011 Gale, Cengage Learning

ALL RIGHTS RESERVED. No part of this work covered by the copyright herein may be reproduced, transmitted, stored, or used in any form or by any means graphic, electronic, or mechanical, including but not limited to photocopying, recording, scanning, digitizing, taping, Web distribution, information networks, or information storage and retrieval systems, except as permitted under Section 107 or 108 of the 1976 United States Copyright Act, without the prior written permission of the publisher.

Since this page cannot legibly accommodate all copyright notices, the acknowledgments constitute an extension of the copyright notice.

For product information and technology assistance, contact us at **Gale Customer Support, 1-800-877-4253.**

For permission to use material from this text or product, submit all requests online at **www.cengage.com/permissions.**

Further permissions questions can be emailed to permissionrequest@cengage.com   While every effort has been made to ensure the reliability of the information presented in this publication, Gale, a part of Cengage Learning, does not guarantee the accuracy of the data contained herein. Gale accepts no payment for listing; and inclusion in the publication of any organization, agency, institution, publication, service, or individual does not imply endorsement of the editors or publisher. Errors brought to the attention of the publisher and verified to the satisfaction of the publisher will be corrected in future editions.

Gale
27500 Drake Rd.
Farmington Hills, MI, 48331-3535

ISBN-13: 978-1-4144-6699-6
ISBN-10: 1-4144-6699-4
ISSN 1094-3552

This title is also available as an e-book.
ISBN-13: 978-1-4144-7365-9
ISBN-10: 1-4144-7365-6

Contact your Gale, a part of Cengage Learning sales representative for ordering information.

The Island of Dr. Moreau

H. G. Wells 1896

Introduction

H. G. Wells and Jules Verne are known as the fathers of science fiction. They helped create the new themes of the genre that carried the Victorian myth of progress into the future. Like the works Wells called his scientific romances, such as *The Time Machine*, *The War of the Worlds, and The Invisible Man*, *The Island of Dr. Moreau* explores the nature of man in light of the science of evolution, relatively new in public consciousness in 1896. Evolution is still at the forefront of the sciences with recent developments in genetics. The field is more controversial than ever as a magnet for calls to reject science by religious fundamentalists, especially by some in America and the Islamic world.

In the novel, Wells draws on ancient myths of animal-human chimeras to create a Swiftian satire about the competing roles of science and religion in society. *The Island of Dr. Moreau* is often imagined in popular culture to be a prediction of genetic engineering, something Wells could hardly have foreseen based on the science of his day. However, what the human imagination conceives, it is usually also eventually able to carry out, though genetic engineering changes living creatures in a way different than the particulars imagined by Wells.

Author Biography

Wells was born on September 21, 1866, in England, to parents who were in domestic service but who had also managed to open a not very successful retail shop. In addition Wells's father played professional cricket, which was also not very lucrative. They intended for Wells to become a draper. However, by reading in the libraries of his mother's employers, Wells educated himself. A primary influence on Wells was his early reading of Plato's *Republic*, which left him with an abiding interest in ideal states and utopias. In his own writing, he often combined that ideal with the Victorian concept of progress.

Due to his self-education, Wells was able to find work as a teacher and attend University College London. There he studied biology under Thomas Huxley, a colleague of Charles Darwin, the most vociferous proponent of the theory of natural selection, commonly known as evolution. In the early 1890s, Wells was incapacitated by tuberculosis and had to resign from teaching (though after a few years the disease became dormant). Wells had actively published in student journals and now began to attempt to earn a living from writing. He had immediate and spectacular success.

Able to support himself and his family as an essayist, Wells found his true métier as a novelist in

1894, when he serialized *The Time Machine*. In this best seller, Wells explored his ideas about evolution, eugenics, class warfare, and socialism in a fantastic futuristic setting. He followed with a number of similar novels, including 1896's *The Island of Dr. Moreau*, which introduced into the mix the newly controversial topic of animal vivisection, and his famous story of space invasion, *The War of the Worlds*, in 1898.

In the first decade of the twentieth century, however, Wells transitioned to a middle period of more realistic novels, such as *Kipps* in 1905, which drew on his experience as a draper's apprentice to explore issues of class. In 1909, his *Ann Veronica* espoused early feminist ideas.

Wells's novels tend to be didactic, a tendency he indulged in book-length essays like *Anticipations* (1901), in which he plainly imagines how technology will have transformed life by the year 2000, and *The Outline of History* (1920), perhaps the most popular of his books during his own lifetime. In old age, he returned to fantastic and utopian themes, most importantly in his novel (1933) and film script (1936) for *Things to Come*. The story depicts a utopian future fulfilling Wells's dream of a single world government, paradoxically made possible by a devastating world war that completely destroys traditional society. Wells continued writing until his eightieth year, when he declined rapidly, dying on August 13, 1946.

Introduction

   The Island of Dr. Moreau begins with an introduction, supposedly written around 1895 by Charles Edward Prendick, who states that the following novel is actually the memoirs of his late uncle Edward. The events described took place in 1887 and 1888, when Edward Prendick's family in England believed him to be lost at sea. Considered mad whenever he tried to speak of what happened during that time, Prendick left a memoir among his papers, found by his nephew. The adventure he had took place on an island near the Galapagos Islands in the South Pacific. Charles Edward believes the only logical island for the setting of his uncle's tale is Noble's Isle (a reference to the noble savage of Jean Jacques Rousseau). Though sailors of the HMS *Scorpion*, visiting in 1891, found nothing unusual, the nephew is willing to vouch for the truth of the story's beginning.

Media Adaptations

- *L'Ile d'Epouvante, released in English as The Island of Terror, was the first film adaptation of The Island of Dr. Moreau.* It was made in France in 1913 and directed by Joë Hamman. Like most films of that era, it appears to be lost.

- *The Island of Dr. Moreau* was adapted in 1932 by Paramount Pictures in the United States as *The Island of Lost Souls*, directed by Erle C. Kenton. Charles Laughton plays Moreau, while Bela Lugosi makes a notable early performance as the Sayer of the Law.

- The 1959 Hollywood film *Terror is a Man*, directed by Gerry de Leon and released by Lynn-Romero

Productions, is a very loose adaptation of *The Island of Dr. Moreau*.

- *The Twilight People*, directed by Eddie Romero in 1972 and produced in the Philippines by Four Associates, is another loose adaptation.

- Joel Stone's experimental play, *Horrors of Dr. Moreau*, was produced in New York in 1972.

- Director Don Taylor's 1977 film *The Island of Dr. Moreau*, produced by American International Pictures and starring Michael York, is one of the best-known adaptations of Wells's novel. This film was further adapted as a comic book written by Doug Monech and drawn by Larry Hama, published by the Marvel Comics Group, also in 1977.

- The most recent film adaptation is director John Frakenheimer's 1996 *The Island of Dr. Moreau*, starring Marlon Brando and produced by New Line Cinema.

Chapter 1: In the Dingey of the Lady Vain

Edward Prendick begins his first-person narrative recalling how the ship he was traveling on, the *Lady Vain*, has sunk. He is cast adrift in a dingy with two of the crew, but no food or water.

After eight days, they agree that one of the three ought to be killed so the others can sustain themselves through cannibalism. One of the sailors is chosen to be the victim by lot. He is unwilling to make the sacrifice, however, and fights another sailor. Both fall overboard into the sea. As Prendick becomes increasingly delirious, he is spotted and rescued by a passing schooner.

Chapter 2: The Man Who Was Going Nowhere

Prendick wakes in a bed in a ship's cabin where he is being tended by a doctor named Montgomery. The doctor is eager for news of London and apparently pleased to find out that Prendick, like himself, has been trained in biology. He seems to have fled from London because of some disgrace he is unwilling to talk about. He tells Prendick that the ship is going on to Hawaii, but only after stopping at the island where Montgomery himself lives.

Chapter 3: The Strange Face

After a few days of recovery, Prendick and Montgomery go up on deck, where a puma and a llama are in a cage, and a brace of hunting hounds are on tethers. The men encounter Montgomery's servant, M'Ling, whom Prendick describes as a black man and the ugliest person he has ever met. There is something about his appearance and mannerisms Prendick seems to recognize but cannot quite put his finger on. Because of his ugliness, M'Ling is hated by the crew of the ship. The drunken Captain Davies physically assaults M'Ling, and Montgomery seems ready to provoke a fight with the captain over the effrontery, but Prendick is able to intervene and keep the peace.

Chapter 4: At the Schooner's Rail

Prendick and the doctor smoke cigars at the ship's rail, observing the volcanic island where Montgomery lives, which is just visible in the distance. Prendick thanks him for saving his life. Montgomery again speaks of the life he had loved in London as a medical student but, he now reveals, he had to abandon because "eleven years ago—I lost my head for ten minutes on a foggy night." This is all the reader learns of Montgomery's secret past.

Chapter 5: The Man Who Had Nowhere to Go

Once they reach the island, Doctor Moreau, as yet unnamed, comes aboard to collect Montgomery and his animal cargo. Prendick expects to go on to Hawaii on the schooner. But Davies, wounded over his earlier intervention to prevent a fight with

Montgomery, forcibly puts Prendick ashore too, though Moreau and Montgomery are reluctant to receive him.

Chapter 6: The Evil-Looking Boatmen

Prendick is towed to the island in the dingy from the *Lady Vain* by a ship that belongs to Moreau, which is crewed by more men whom Prendick is at a loss to characterize. He comments on their ugliness, and mentions how strange their movements and the proportions of their bodies are. Moreau welcomes Prendick, explaining to him they might not see another ship for a year. He questions him about his education and takes some interest in the fact that Prendick has studied biology with Thomas Huxley (the same education Wells had). He explains that the island is essentially a biological research station. Moreau and Montgomery busy themselves in releasing several dozen rabbits that are among the animals left by the ship. They wish the rabbits to become feral and breed a population of game animals.

Chapter 7: The Locked Door

Prendick is given a room in the compound occupied by Moreau and Montgomery. Moreau tells him that his work is secret and he can hardly share it with a stranger, whatever his scientific training, until he is better known. Hence Prendick is locked out of the laboratory. When Prendick overhears the name Moreau for the first time, he remembers a scandal from some years previous in which an undercover journalist got himself hired by Moreau as an assistant. The man exposed Moreau's practice of vivisection, causing a public scandal that drove Moreau, a prominent scientist, out of the country. Prendick begins to wonder about the connection between the notorious vivisectionist and the deformed and hideous men who inhabit the island.

Chapter 8: The Crying of the Puma

Over lunch, Prendick challenges Montgomery with the fact that M'Ling has pointed, furry ears. Montgomery disingenuously pretends surprise. Moreau is absent and, from the terrible screaming of the puma left by the ship, Prendick deduces that Moreau is vivisecting it. Tormented by its terrible cries, "as if all the pain in the world had found a voice," Prendick walks outside to get away from it.

Chapter 9: The Thing in the Forest

Walking away from the compound, Prendick comes upon a stream where he observes one of the characteristically deformed men of the island getting down on all fours to drink water like an animal. When the man notices he's been observed, he gives Prendick a guilty look, then runs off. Prendick next finds the body of a rabbit with its head torn off. He then secretly observes three of the inhabitants singing and dancing. He realizes for the first time the odd thing that he could never pin down. Though they are undeniably human in appearance, however grotesque, the familiar thing about them is that they are reminiscent of animals—in this case, pigs.

Prendick realizes that it is dusk and decides it would be better not to remain in the forest with these creatures, whatever they are, after dark. He returns to the compound but is followed, then chased, by the same Thing (as he calls it) that he saw drinking. Finally he uses his handkerchief as a sling to knock it unconscious with a rock.

Chapter 10: The Crying of the Man

When Prendick returns and meets Montgomery, he demands to know if he was chased by a man or an animal. Montgomery suggests it was a phantom of Prendick's own fear. He gives Prendick a sleeping draught that Prendick, exhausted, is glad to take. The next morning, Prendick wakes to Montgomery rushing through the locked door to the laboratory. He is in such a hurry that he leaves the door unlocked. When Prendick hears screams that do not come from a puma but a person, he goes through the door, and sees Moreau vivisecting what appears to be a human being. The physically large and powerful Moreau throws him out and locks the door. Prendick hears him arguing with Montgomery about what they ought to do with him.

Chapter 11: The Hunting of the Man

Prendick deduces from what he has seen that Moreau is not only vivisecting human beings, but that he has devised some method to turn men into beasts. When he opens his outside door just as Montgomery seems about to lock him in, Prendick becomes convinced that Moreau intends to torture and experiment on him and makes a run for it into the jungle surrounding the compound. Chased by Montgomery, who has a pistol and is tracking him with a dog, Prendick meets one of the island's inhabitants (whom he calls Beast People). The creature is part human, part ape. Prendick persuades the Beast Person to take him to the village where the creatures made by Moreau live.

Chapter 12: The Sayers of the Law

Prendick finds that the Beast People worship Moreau and consider him a law-giver. He is forced by the Sayer of the Law to repeat a litany of Moreau's laws against animalistic behavior and then a liturgy of praise for Moreau as creator. Finally Moreau and Montgomery arrive with guns and dogs and order the Beast People to capture Prendick. He manages to elude them and leads them on another wild chase through the jungle. Prendick is trying to reach the sea, where he hopes to drown himself rather than submit to the torture he fears at the hands of Moreau.

Chapter 13: The Parley

Once Moreau has Prendick cornered in the ocean, Prendick starts to shout out, talking to the Beast People directly, that Moreau has been turning men into animals and that he doesn't understand why they don't take revenge when they could very easily kill their tormenters. Moreau manages to shout him down and explains to him (in very broken school boy Latin so the Beast People will not understand), "*Hi non sunt homines; sunt animalia qui nos habemus*—vivisected." The Beast People are not men turned into animals as Prendick believes, but rather animals Moreau has turned into human beings. Montgomery and Moreau convince Prendick that he is in no danger, partially through reason, but mainly by a show of good faith, giving him their guns.

Chapter 14: Doctor Moreau Explains

Back at the compound, Moreau explains to Prendick what he has been doing to his animal subjects. Wells's technique in this section is to move from known premises step-by-step toward the fantastic. (Moreau's technique seems far more fantastic today to the extent science has discovered how much more complex living beings are than was imagined in the 1890s.) Moreau begins by reminding Prendick that reconstructive surgery (such as making a new nose for an accident victim) is possible, as are other surgical modifications.

While other scientists feared to go far in this direction because of ethical concerns, Moreau proceeded dispassionately and discovered nearly unlimited potential for such techniques. He is able to take any animal and reshape its skeleton and muscles to human form, and is also able to change the very nature of its organs (including the brain).

Grafting and transfusions between species play an important part in Moreau's work. He is able to create a human consciousness in his transformed animals through techniques like hypnosis. But eventually, Moreau always fails, because as soon as he done, the subjects start to revert back to their animal nature. Prendick objects that the pain the animals suffer through vivisection does not seem worth its outcome. Moreau replies that pain is a useless evolutionary vestige that humanity must overcome. He claims that the religion practiced by the Beast People is their own invention based on evangelizing they experienced from human servants he kept on the island years ago.

Chapter 15: Concerning the Beast Folk

Montgomery introduces Prendick to the Beast People. The most intelligent of them was originally a gorilla. Others were made from pigs. Many are hybrids, like the Fox-bear woman and Montgomery's servant M'ling, who is a Bear-dog. The crew of Moreau's boat were originally bulls, and there is even a Rhinoceros-mare. The most dangerous are the Leopard-man (the one that stalked Prendick through the forest) and the Hyena-swine. Some of them are able to breed, and if they bear live young they are wholly animal, but Moreau immediately goes to work vivisecting them. There are about seventy remaining Beast People of about 120 Moreau created during his eleven years on the island.

Chapter 16: How the Beast Folk Taste Blood

While walking in the forest, Prendick and Montgomery encounter the partially eaten body of a rabbit. This alarms Montgomery and alarms Moreau more when they tell him. It means one of the Beast People is breaking the law. They rush to the village to investigate. When Moreau asks which of the Beast People has broken the law against eating flesh, the Leopard-man attacks Moreau and runs off into the forest. The three men and the Beast People give chase and Prendick and the Hyena-swine happen to find the fugitive. Rather than allow Moreau to torture the creature through more vivisection, Prendick shoots and kills it. But at almost the same instant he fires, the Hyena-swine attacks its throat. This causes Prendick to believe that the Hyena-swine was the rabbit killer all along.

Chapter 17: A Catastrophe

Eight or more weeks later, when Prendick is

taking the air outside the compound, he hears the puma scream as usual under Moreau's vivisection. Suddenly, the partially humanized puma, swathed in bandages, comes rushing past him, knocking him down and breaking his arm. Moreau follows, and Montgomery follows, stopping long enough to examine Prendick's arm. Left alone all day, Prendick occasionally hears gunshots from the jungle. In the afternoon, Montgomery returns, explaining that he never found Moreau but had to shoot several of the Beast People when they attacked him, a thing that has never happened before.

Chapter 18: The Finding of Moreau

After Montgomery attends to Prendick's arm, they set out again to search for Moreau. They find a group of Beast People who have evidently seen his corpse. Thinking quickly, and fearful that their animal natures might lead them to attack if they are no longer controlled by fear of Moreau, Prendick assures them that Moreau is not dead but has left his body to go into the sky where he can watch them better, and that someday he will return. They indeed find Moreau's body and that of the puma who apparently killed him. The puma herself, although she has a gunshot wound, has been partially eaten. They take Moreau's body back to the compound and lock themselves in for the night. They euthanize the animals Moreau had in various states of vivisection.

Chapter 19: Montgomery's Bank Holiday

In Britain, a bank holiday is similar to a federal holiday in the United states. It is used in chapter 19 to mean an unrestrained celebration. Drunk, Montgomery becomes agitated when Prendick suggests they have to somehow get back to the mainland. Since Montgomery is evidently wanted for a crime in England, he does not feel that he can return to civilization. He decides to go to the Beast People and get them drunk. The next day, Prendick is planning to set out in Moreau's boat when he hears a terrible commotion coming from the beach. Prendick finds that Montgomery and the Sayer of the Law have killed each other. M'Ling is also dead. Montgomery had the Beast People destroy the boat and turn the wood into a bonfire, determined that if he could not go back to the world, then Prendick would not go either. Prendick finds that in his rush to get to the beach, he knocked over a kerosene lamp, burning down the compound.

Chapter 20: Alone with the Beast People

At dawn Prendick, still by the dead bodies on the beach, is approached by three Beast People. He has the presence of mind to forestall any attack by overawing them, cracking his whip and acting like Moreau. He gives them orders to dump the bodies in the ocean. When the Hyena-swine comes,

Prendick immediately tries to kill him, but misses his pistol shot and is too exhausted to give chase when the creature runs into the jungle. Prendick goes off by himself to consider what to do, but to little purpose, and then goes to the Beast People's village. At last he succumbs to sleep.

Chapter 21: The Reversion of the Beast Folk

Prendick gains a loyal companion in a Beast-man who had originally been a Saint-Bernard. Prendick is able to convince most of the Beast-People to continue their worship of Moreau, which he considers a means of protecting himself through the Law's prohibition of murder. He instructs the Saint-Bernard-man to kill the Hyena-swine on sight. Not very adept at carpentry, Prendick builds a raft over many months of labor. During this time the Beast People all revert with increasing rapidity to their animal natures, losing the power of speech, the ability to walk upright, and other human characteristics. The Saint-Bernard-man finally fights the Hyena-swine and is killed, but Prendick is able to shoot the Hyena-swine, the most dangerous of Moreau's creatures. Shortly thereafter, a small ship drifts ashore on the island, containing two dead bodies. One of them, Prendick suggests, may be Captain Davies of the *Ipecacuanha*. Prendick sees how lucky he is to escape before the reverting Beast People inevitably kill him.

Chapter 22: The Man Alone

Prendick is eventually rescued and returned to England. He finds it impossible to fit back into human society. He cannot shake the feeling that all the people he sees on the streets of London are really Beast People on the verge of degenerating into animals. Prendick tells his story to the captain of the ship that rescued him, who can't believe it, considering it delirium produced by the castaway's ordeal. Prendick eventually finds some help by talking to a psychiatrist who knew Moreau years before. Prendick finally retires to a country house and devotes himself to studying the unchanging perfection of the stars.

Note

In this brief epilogue, Wells creates himself as a character and assures the reader that, however fantastic they seem, the technical details of vivisection presented in the story are true.

Captain John Davies

Davies is the owner and captain of the *Ipecacuanha*, the ship that rescues Prendick from the lifeboat. He is also transporting animal specimens to Moreau's island. He is an alcoholic who has lost his master's license. While he is incompetent and difficult, Moreau or Montgomery no doubt chose him because he would be in no position to call for official inquiries regarding anything he might accidentally find out about Moreau's research.

Fox-bear

The Fox-bear is a female of the Beast People.

Hyena-swine

The Hyena-swine is the most dangerous of Moreau's Beast People. Although it is feral, in the sense of returning to its animal habits before any of its fellows, it is made from a pig, an animal that has many startling similarities to human beings. The pig is often used to characterize the worst human traits, especially in Wells's day; to call someone "Swine!" was a deadly insult, however old-fashioned it might seem today. This disposition is combined with the hyena, arguably a more violent and effective predator than a lion or tiger. The Hyena-swine is so dangerous, perhaps, not because it is the least human of the Beast People but because it is the most human in its rejection of authority and rebellion against conformity. In any case, after Moreau's death, Prendick's chief concern, save only escape from the island, is to hunt down and kill the Hyena-swine. He views it as an existential threat in a way that none of the other Beast People, even those made from predators such as wolves, are.

Leopard-Man

The Leopard-man is another dangerous Beast Person. He stalks Prendick, and one of the chief causes of Moreau's difficulties in managing the Beast People is the necessity of controlling the Leopard-man's feral instincts. Nevertheless, many of the transgressions of the Law the Leopard-man is accused of may actually have been performed by the Hyena-swine.

M'Ling

M'Ling is Montgomery's servant who accompanied him on the voyage from the mainland with the new specimens. He was originally a bear grafted with elements of a dog. Montgomery treats him exactly the same way people treat dogs, playing with him, petting him, and talking soothing gibberish to him. But when Montgomery is drunk, he abuses M'Ling horribly, beating him and frightening him with fire crackers. Like a dog, M'Ling remains affectionate and obedient anyway. When Montgomery is eventually attacked by the Beast People, M'Ling fights and dies trying to protect him.

Montgomery

Montgomery is a physician who works as Moreau's assistant. He also tends to Prendick after he is rescued from the lifeboat and is the first person Prendick sees on regaining consciousness. He is "a youngish man with flaxen hair, a bristly straw-coloured moustache and a dropping nether lip." He studied biology at University College London and thus shares some of the same background as Wells. Montgomery shows his violent and uncontrolled temper on the voyage to the island. He works with Moreau because a terrible disgrace he committed, which is never explained, has driven him from civilization. Despite Prendick's gratitude to Montgomery for saving his life more than once, the two men are never able to form a friendship. Montgomery is an alcoholic, and his reaction to Moreau's death is to become drunk and then to introduce the Beast People to alcohol. He is killed during this celebration by the Sayer of the Law, perhaps because his lawlessness was more than the overwhelmed creature could take.

Doctor Moreau

The name Moreau is French, and by a pun, it

can be interpreted as a combination of the French words for *death* and *water*. This interpretation gains importance given that in Wells's earlier novel, *The Time Machine*, Wells's name for the more bestial of the two species of human beings the Time Traveler finds in the future, "Mor-lock," could have the same meaning (*lock* or *loch* is a dialectical word for lake). The name thus equates death and, using water as a symbol, life. In both cases, the goals of the name bearer are futile. The name Moreau may also be meant to recall Gustave Moreau, the leading French painter of Wells's era, whose most famous painting is *Oedipus and the Sphinx* (1874), rendering a monster with the head of a beautiful woman and the body of a lion.

When Prendick first sees Moreau, he describes the doctor as "a massive white-haired man in dirty-blue flannels." When Prendick hears the name Moreau, he recalls him as "a prominent and masterful physiologist, well-known in scientific circles for his extraordinary imagination and his brutal directness in discussion," a description that could apply equally to Wells's teacher Huxley.

Moreau is on a quest. His first purpose is primarily scientific. He explains to Prendick, "You see, I went on with this research just the way that it led me. That is the only way I ever heard of true research going. I asked a question, devised some method of obtaining an answer, and got—a fresh question." But, Moreau is also insane: although he claims to have happened upon the human form as the target of his operations by chance and does not think that evolution leads upward from the beast to the human as a teleological goal, he departs from science entirely when he claims to know that evolution is leading in the direction of eliminating pain, and moreover claims to be doing the work of evolution by way of justifying the pain inflicted on his animal subjects. Moreau imagines that he, an ordinary human being, is acting on an equal footing with natural law. He is no longer aware of his own mortality.

Charles Edward Prendick

The author of the introduction, Charles Edward Prendick is the nephew of Edward Prendick and the supposed editor and publisher of his uncle's memoirs.

Edward Prendick

Prendick is the main character and narrator of *The Island of Dr. Moreau*. He is a young man of independent means who takes up the study of natural history (as biological science was then called). He takes a voyage in the South Seas to study relatively untouched and unexplored natural environments as Darwin did, and indeed as his (and Wells's) teacher Huxley had done. However, his motives are not noble but comic: he was bored and rich and had nothing better to do. Taken by chance to Moreau's Noble's Isle, he is confronted with new and nearly unimaginable circumstances. His character is designed by Wells to be one whose inner life will not distract the reader from the dramatic thread of the narrative, though at the same time he does undergo realistic transformations of character.

If Moreau is the anti-hero of the novel, it would nevertheless be difficult to call Prendick the hero. He constantly adapts himself to his circumstances and, by a series of lucky chances, survives, fulfilling the evolutionary process. But Prendick fails as a scientist. Given the chance to use inductive reasoning to predict what Moreau is doing in his experiments, he reasons in too constrained and pedestrian a manner and guesses wrongly that Moreau is turning human beings into animals. This leads to a gothic horror story conjured up out of Prendick's imagination that the reader, following Prendick, must follow. But Moreau makes up for Prendick's defective reasoning and explains to both Prendick and the reader that really, since Moreau is turning beasts into human beings, Prendick is rather experiencing a satiric horror story of a more nearly theological character, like *Frankenstein*.

Puma

The Puma is first introduced as a caged animal on the deck of the *Ipecacuanha* on its way to Moreau's island. It escapes while still being vivisected, presumably still fully animal in its intellect. It kills Moreau, who succeeded in shooting it during the death struggle. It is also attacked, and perhaps finally killed, by the Hyena-swine.

Rhinoceros-mare

The Rhinoceros-mare is a female of the Beast People.

Saint-Bernard-man

One of Moreau's Beast Men had originally been a Saint-Bernard dog. He retains even more dog-like characteristics than M'Ling. After Moreau's death, when all of the other animals begin to reject the dominance hierarchy that Moreau established over them, the Saint-Bernard-man is anxious merely to find a new master and happily accepts Prendick in that role. As the Beast People revert to their animal nature, the Saint-Bernard's loyalty to Prendick does not wane, and on Prendick's orders, he fights, and is eventually killed by, the Hyena-swine.

Sayer of the Law

The Sayer of the Law is the head of the Beast People and leads them in the litany of the Law handed down to them by Moreau. His hands are misshapen like hooves and he is covered in gray hair. Prendick thinks he may have originally been a kind of deer. He does little throughout the novel but constantly repeat the Law. Finally, however, perhaps because he feels a special depth of betrayal when Moreau's death signals the Law's falsity, he turns on his human master Montgomery during a drunken, lawless celebration, kills the man, and is fatally shot himself in the struggle.

Evolution (Biology)

On the first page of *The Island of Dr. Moreau,* Wells establishes the groundwork for the evolutionary context for his novel. Moreau's Noble's Isle is located near the Galapagos Islands, where Darwin famously did his field work. There, Darwin noticed the special adaptations of the islands' finches, tortoises, and other animals to very specific biological niches. Moreover, Prendick, before his shipwreck, set out to study natural history (as evolutionary biology was then called). His interrupted voyage is modeled on Darwin's famous cruise on the HMS *Beagle*, as well as on the similar research expedition undertaken by Darwin's follower Thomas Huxley to New Guinea and Australia on the HMS *Rattlesnake* (perhaps the model for the HMS *Scorpion* Wells has survey Noble's Isle).

Wells studied biology with Thomas Huxley, who, after Darwin, was the leading proponent of evolutionary science in Victorian Britain. It is not a surprise, then, that one of the things *The Island of Dr. Moreau* encompasses is an intimate conversation on the subject with Huxley's "Prolegomena" to *Evolution and Ethics* from 1893. In this essay, Huxley makes a case that human beings, since the beginning of civilization, have been removed from the natural selection that drives evolutionary adaptation. Evolution is essentially the changing of species over time to better fit their environment. The change comes from the selection of variations within a population of those individuals best fitted to their circumstance: they will have more successful offspring and pass on more genetic information to the next generation. But human beings, according to Huxley, are no longer subject to predation—living solely off of hunting prey—and in general not to starvation, so everyone has an equal chance to pass on their genetic inheritance. Individual fitness is no longer an issue. When human beings do react to environmental pressures—for example, famine—it is not by the change of the genetic make-up of populations but by concerted social action. It is society, not individuals, that evolves now. In short, the bodies of human beings are not like other organisms living in a state of nature subject to evolutionary pressure but like the inhabitants of a garden carefully protected from competition and evolutionary pressure.

Modern scientists would no doubt hasten to add many caveats to the margins of Huxley's analysis, such as genetic resistances to disease as a selective force, however sound the general point is. Competition for the basic necessities of life no longer exists among human beings, and competition within the society that guarantees access to those resources is instead to fulfill desires, to avoid pain, and to experience pleasure at an individual level.

Moreau, in contrast, has a distorted view of evolution. He believes that human beings are evolving in a specific pre-determined direction, namely to lose the ability to feel pain, and more generally to replace feeling of all kinds with reason. This may somehow be the larger background of his experiments. But, of course, evolution shapes organisms to their immediate circumstances, and does not aim for any specific teleological goal to attain in the future. But Moreau's confusion is deeper, because what he is doing is the opposite of evolution, as Huxley explains it:

> The tendency of the cosmic process [evolution] is to bring about the adjustment of the forms of plant life to the current conditions; the tendency of the horticultural process is the adjustment of the conditions to the needs of the forms of plant life which the gardener desires to raise.

Moreau is playing the role of the gardener by shaping his Beast People to his own ends, not those of nature to which evolution had already shaped them. The monstrosity of Moreau consists in his imagining himself playing an even grander role than that of the gardener in Huxley's scheme. As a thought experiment, Huxley imagines human beings, instead of being freed from selection by culture, instead subject to the same kind of selection that the gardener makes, killing weeds and uprooting plants whose flowers fail to please him: "Let us now imagine that some administrative authority, as far superior in power and intelligence to men, as men are to their cattle, is set over [human society]." Moreau imagines himself to be exactly such an authority, in that he is reshaping not merely human society but nature itself through his operations.

Topics for Further Study

- It is a common motif of steampunk literature—speculative fiction that uses steam-era technology in science-fictional ways—to depict Dr. Moreau using biological warfare against the Martians that invade the earth in Wells's *The War of The Worlds*. In both Alan Moore's comic book *The League of Extraordinary Gentlemen* and in the young-adult novel *The Martian War* by Kevin J. Anderson (writing under the pseudonym Gabriel Mesta), Moreau does so at the behest of the British government. But what if Moreau were left to his own devices during the chaos created by the Martian invasion? What if he had to turn for help to whoever was nearest at hand, say the population of another South Seas island? What if Moreau had to use the aid of the multi-cultural utopia described in the novel *The Island* by Aldous Huxley (grandson of Wells's teacher Thomas Huxley)? Read at least one of these sources and write a short story about Moreau's confrontation with a different culture in a time of crisis. Points to consider include how Moreau's philosophy might be changed by his contact with the islanders, or how Moreau would be viewed by another culture.

- Use the Internet to research the historical introduction of rabbits into island environments, especially Australia. Create a multimedia presentation suggesting how Moreau's introduction of rabbits onto Noble's Isle might have affected the ecology there.

- Wells used the concepts of evolution and creation in a very complex way to illustrate his beliefs about religion. This topic was already controversial in 1860 when Thomas Huxley debated against Archbishop Wilber-force. How is evolution used in such debates today? Both YouTube and TedTalks have video records of hundreds of debates between scientists and church and political leaders on this topic. Use clips from these debates to illustrate a class presentation on the topic.

- The boundary between the human and nonhuman is a main theme of many novels of the late 1800s, including not only *The Island of Dr. Moreau* but also *Dr. Jekyll and Mr. Hyde* by Robert Louis Stevenson, *The Great God Pan* by Arthur Machen, and *Dracula* by Bram Stoker. Write a paper comparing the various approaches taken and conclusions reached by some of these books regarding human and nonhuman interaction.

Racism

Racism was pervasive in the nineteenth century in a way that can hardly be imagined today. Even the most progressive proponents of the abolition of slavery and of the equality of rights for all human beings, such as Abraham Lincoln and Thomas Huxley, did not think that what they called different races of men were equal in intellect and other areas of life. The superiority that Western European countries and the United States enjoyed in the system of colonization was taken as proof that the men of those cultures were also superior. In fact, however, modern biological science does not acknowledge the existence of race as a scientific category, since there has been no significant isolation of human groups since the last common ancestor of all human beings, known as mitochondrial Eve, about 70,000 years ago. The equality of achievement among human beings from all parts of the world makes the falsity of distinctions based on arbitrary racial categories obvious.

Wells did not depart from the common racist attitudes of his day, and racism is clear in *The Island of Dr. Moreau*. One of the things that makes Prendick nervous about the Beast People when he first encounters them is that he is unable to fit them into his pre-conceived racial categories. Moreau is equally enmeshed in racism when he describes his first successful experiment: "Then I took a gorilla I had; and upon that, working with infinite care and mastering difficulty after difficulty, I made my first man…. I thought him a fair specimen of the negroid type when I had finished him." The statement implies that black Africans are closer to being animals than other human beings.

But Wells's pre-conceived notions prevent him from taking mere facts into account. The Beast People have their own racism, no doubt imposed on them by Moreau's hypnotic indoctrination. They judge each other by how closely their hands approximate a human hand, so the Ape-man thinks himself superior to his fellows. This embraces the core racist fantasy: that there is an ideal human type and each human individual is to be measured against that as being closer to the human or the animal. But biological science makes it plain that there is not an ideal type of any organism, and that fitness of a species consists in the widest possible diversity.

Science Fiction

Science fiction did not exist as a genre in Wells's day, nor, indeedd did the phrase. He called his fantastic stories scientific romances. Wells is often paired with his older contemporary, French novelist Jules Verne, as the fathers, or precursors, of science fiction. While Verne was interested in describing emergent technology, Wells's premises are usually utterly fantastic. Jorge Luis Borges summed up the difference between them precisely when, in his obituary of Wells (translated in Parrinder's collection of Wells Criticism) he has Verne apocryphally exclaim of Wells, "*Il invente!*" ("He's making it up!").

More seriously, Wells was concerned with how science could be applied to reshape human society. *The Time Machine* and *The War of the Worlds* show what might happen if society were not reformed on scientific lines. Most of his other novels show science in charge, no matter how fantastic the means of it getting there. *In the Days of the Comet*, the means is a gas that makes everyone in the world think rationally, while in *Things to Come*, scientists rebuild the world after a devastating war destroys civilization. *The Island of Dr. Moreau* fits into this category with its message favoring eugenics, the practice of improving human or animal stock through selective breeding.

Wells's utopian and dystopian themes were taken up by the next generation of British novelists, such as Aldous Huxley in *Brave New World* and George Orwell in *1984*, and by more recent authors, notably Margaret Atwood. Though in his later life, Wells discounted his early scientific romances in favor of more purely sociological projects, there is no doubt his popularity and lasting fame are based on these very works.

The Education Act of 1870, a reaction to the fear that Britain might lose its scientific and industrial supremacy to a rising Germany just victorious in the Franco-Prussian War, provided for extensive scholarship funds to educate young men of the lower classes in science. This not only was the source of Wells's own education but also provided a large scientifically literate readership for Wells's new Scientific Romances.

Documentary Novel

The Island of Dr. Moreau is a novel and therefore wholly fictitious, but Wells strains every nerve to make his narrative voices suggest otherwise to the reader. The main text of the novel is narrated by Charles Prendick. It is written completely in the form of a memoir rather than a novel. This form gives the reader an expectation of truthfulness on the part of the narrator. The expectation is supported by an introduction supposedly written by Prendick's nephew, attesting to the genuineness of the main text as a manuscript written by his uncle and left to him for publication. The nephew even describes his research into ships's registries, travel schedules, and other records to verify the story as far as humanly possible. In short, Wells gives his fiction verisimilitude by casting it precisely in the form of genres that are ordinarily accepted as true.

Wells is not trying to trick his readers by any means, but the form allows the reader an added excitement by allowing him to pretend that the work is true. This relates to what the romantic poet Samuel Taylor Coleridge called the willing suspension of disbelief: that when a fantastic narrative is brought before the reader, the author must beguile the reader's objections to keep him from thinking about how patently false it is. Throughout the twentieth century, critics held this suspension to be a vital element of the science fiction genre, which necessarily deals in fantastic subject matter. In later times, the original concept was somewhat misunderstood, with critics acting as if it meant the reader had to give up skepticism.

Wells returns to lending fictional credibility to his narrative in his final Note, where he apparently speaks in his own voice to assure the reader that he has already published many of the substantive ideas of the novel in non-fiction, didactic essays. He states, "There can be no denying that, whatever amount of credibility attaches to the detail of this story, the manufacture of monsters—and perhaps even of quasi-human monsters—is within the possibilities of vivisection." Wells reassures the reader of the truth of what he full well knows not to be the truth: the very essence of fiction.

The use of fictitious documentary forms to create verisimilitude was a specialty of popular novelists of the 1880s and 1890s, though it has since fallen out of favor. Compare the elaborate efforts of Conan Doyle to place Watson the memoirist as a screen between his fictions of Sherlock Holmes and the reader. Bram Stoker's *Dracula* (1897) is also composed of letters, transcripts of meetings, and other documentary forms. If Wells can be said to have a particular model in mind for *The Island of Dr. Moreau*, it is Swift's *Gulliver's Travels*, another pseudo-memoir.

Although Wells and his generation were not aware of it, this use of non-fiction forms to provide verisimilitude for fiction harkens back to the birth of the novel as the romances of the Roman Empire. Roman aristocrats were trained at a university level in rhetoric, and most of their advanced course work consisted in producing sample documents: administrative letters, political speeches, trial summations, and so forth. Since these were merely for the sake of perfecting the form, students were free to invent any substantive details they wished. In other words, they wrote fictive versions of real documentary forms. The art of purposefully writing fictions and finally the novel perhaps grew directly out of this work.

Vivisection

As modern surgical techniques were developed throughout the nineteenth century, it became possible to examine the functioning of living systems, rather than merely studying anatomy through dissection of dead specimens. This practice led to important and continuing advances in medical science, with life-saving results for millions of human beings. Such operations are called vivisection, meaning surgery on living specimens. Criticism of vivisection was immediately offered on the grounds that some animals that are vivisected are ultimately killed or otherwise suffer harm. Organized opposition to vivisection formed around groups like the Theosophical Society, which opposed the practice in accord with ancient Pythagorean and Vedic religious teachings relating to reincarnation.

The popular press was anxious to promote views opposing vivisection since the dramatic portrayal of animal experiments as acts of cruelty performed by sadistic men (despite the fact that the scientists who work with animals are generally more concerned about their welfare than anyone, for practical as much as ethical reasons) were sensationalistic and sold newspapers. Even the reputation of the fictional Doctor Moreau fell to such a newspaper campaign. Wells himself fully exploited, in *The Island of Doctor Moreau*, the sensationalism associated with vivisection in 1890s England.

But despite Wells's constant use of the term "vivisection," Moreau's techniques not only have nothing to do with real vivisection but they are not even physically possible. It is clear from their constant screams that Moreau's subjects are conscious during his operations. But any animal undergoing surgery has to be anesthetized; otherwise it would not be possible to restrain them securely enough to prevent their movements, making surgery impossible. Any animal (or for that matter a human being) undergoing major surgery without anesthetic would die of shock very quickly, as Wells very well knew.

Eugenics

Like many intellectuals of his generation, Wells embraced the originally American pseudo-science of eugenics. This is the belief that positive steps should be taken to improve the genetic characteristics of human beings. Wells feared that, since evolutionary pressures for the most part do not operate on human beings, they would be subject to evolutionary degeneration, with nothing to weed out any newly appearing bad traits. This is clearly the message of his novel *The Time Machine*, which depicts a future in which the Homo sapiens species has split into two species, both of them barely sentient. One is incapable of defending itself and the other is cannibalistic. Wells stated his views plainly in the *American Journal of Sociology* in 1904:

> I believe that now and always the conscious selection of the best for reproduction will be impossible: that to propose it is to display a fundamental misunderstanding of what individuality implies. The way of nature has always been to slay the hindmost, and there is still no other way, unless we can prevent those who would become the hindmost being born. It is in the sterilization of failures, and not in the selection of successes for breeding, that the possibility of an improvement of the human stock lies.

With the events of the Holocaust still in the future, it must have been difficult for Wells to imagine the enormity of what he was proposing. He may well have believed that he was following the dictates of his teacher Huxley. But Huxley's famous "Prolegomena" is essentially an argument against eugenics, for Huxley there says, "There is no hope that mere human beings will ever possess enough intelligence to select the fittest." This might seem to agree with Wells's statement. But Huxley goes on to observe that selecting the fit and the unfit is exactly the same process, and that either is equally impossible.

It was also evident to Huxley that no program

of eugenics could possibly be put into practice without the disastrous, society-destroying, consequences that would be realized in the Holocaust: "I do not see how such selection could be practiced without a serious weakening, it may be the destruction, of the bonds which hold society together." Huxley also demonstrates conclusively that the criticism, made both then and now, that evolutionary science somehow leads to eugenics, is false. The fantasies of the eugenicist are the opposite of evolutionary science. Their actions do not conform to natural selection, as they think, but rather are like the action of a gardener, pulling out native plants to protect their favored species that are too maladapted to their environment to survive on their own. Eugenics could in no sense "improve" the genetic character of a species (a concept that has no meaning in biological science), but would rather serve to decrease its diversity and therefore its ability to adapt to changes in environment, making it less fit from an evolutionary viewpoint.

Compare & Contrast

- **1890s:** Vivisection, a relatively new phenom enon in medical science, is a controversial issue exploited by the press.

  Today: Vivisection, and more generally experimentation on living animals, despite a proven track record of contribution to life-saving research, is still highly controversial.

- **1890s:** Evolution, already firmly established as the basis of biology, is highly controversial in Britain because of perceived conflicts with religion.

  Today: Religious opposition to biological science is led by fundamentalists among the Islamic immigrant community in Britain.

- **1890s:** Racism is pervasive and easily accepted in society.

  Today: Racial discrimination is outlawed in Britain, a world leader in multicultural education.

- **1890s:** Essential transformation of animal physiology is essentially fantasy.

  Today: Developments in genetic science have made the manipulation of living organisms commonplace (for example, cloning of animals), though there seems to be little reason to bridge animal to human forms in the way Moreau attempted.

Huxley's disproof of eugenics notwithstanding, Wells wove eugenic themes into *The Island of Dr. Moreau* as well as *The Time Machine*. The Beast

People Moreau creates constantly undergo reversion to their animal condition unless Moreau works on them to keep them human. This is a symbolic expression of Wells's irrational fear that humanity will revert to an animal condition if natural selection is not replaced by some kind of artificial eugenic selection. The veil of symbolism lifts when Prendick returns to London and says, "I could not persuade myself that the men and women I met … would [not] presently begin to revert, to show first this bestial mark and then that."

Critical Overview

Coming soon after the best-selling success of *The Time Machine*, *The Island of Dr. Moreau* was widely reviewed in the British press. Many of the reviews are collected in Patrick Parrinder's anthology *H. G. Wells: The Critical Heritage*. Critics generally reacted to the title as a sensational exploitation of vivisection. This is well expressed in a review from the *Speaker* of April 18, 1896, that was included in *H. G. Wells: The Critical Heritage* :

> Mr. Wells ... has talent, and he employs it here for a purpose which is absolutely degrading. It is no excuse that he should have made his book one that sends a thrill of horror though the mind of the reader. After all, even among writers of fiction, talents are accompanied by responsibilities—a fact which Mr. Wells seems to have forgotten.

Another complaint was that a literal understanding of Moreau's technique was physically impossible. Wells (in an essay reprinted in appendix 6 in the edition of the novel edited by Robert M. Philmus titled *The Island of Doctor Moreau: A Variorum Text* went to some lengths to defend this. He cites current scientific papers that seem to suggest inter-species transplantation and grafting are possible. But any such hints were never confirmed. The rejection response by the immune system, which was hardly even suspected in 1896, makes any such transplantation impossible.

Literary scholars have largely rejected these early lines of criticism and found some interesting new lines of interpretation. Peter Kemp, for instance, in *H. G. Wells and the Culminating Ape*, doubts the hopefulness many scholars find in Prendick's final turn to astronomy on account of this, too, leading to disaster and bloodshed in *The War of the Worlds* with its invasion of the earth by Martians. Steven McLean, in his *Early Fictions of H. G. Wells*, makes something out of a stray remark of Wells's that part of the inspiration for *The Island of Dr. Moreau* was Oscar Wilde's trial for sodomy (then a crime in England) in the spring of 1895. In that case, Moreau's recreation of his animals into men through pain stands for the gratuitous punishment the state inflicted on Wilde in order to correct him into something society arrogantly regarded as superior to his own nature.

Something should also be said about the text of the novel itself. Unusual for a modern, widely published novel, two different critical editions of the text of *The Island of Dr. Moreau* were published in the 1990s. The Philmus edition is based on the first American publication of *The Island of Dr. Moreau* by Stone and Kimball in May of 1896. The text edited by Leon Stover, on the other hand, is based on a British edition that Heinemann published in April of 1896. The American edition is not in any sense a simple reprint of the British. Rather, both seem to have been based on a largely finished typescript (not now extant) that Wells supplied to the publisher. Each then had different handwritten annotations, or different changes agreed with the publisher through correspondence. Wells could have decided the matter when the text was reprinted in the so-called Atlantic edition of his early novels in 1924. But by then Wells held his early scientific romances in some disdain and evidently allowed a friend, novelist Dorothy Richardson, to oversee the extensive changes in that text. Most mass market reprints of *The Island of Dr. Moreau* are based on this later text, but this discussion uses Philmus's edition.

What Do I Read Next?

- *The League of Extraordinary Gentlemen* is a comic book series begun in 1999 by writer Alan Moore and illustrator Kevin O'Neil. It takes place in Edwardian London and features characters, including Doctor Moreau and Edward Prendick, from several novels and stories of that era written by H. G. Wells, Arthur Conan Doyle, Jules Verne, Bram Stoker, H. Rider Haggard, and other writers.

- Richard Consta's *H. G. Wells*, revised in 1985 for Twayne's English Authors Series, provides a general introduction to Wells and his writing.

- *Fruits Basket*, a young-adult manga series by Natsuki Takaya serialized in Japan from 1999 through 2006 and published in U.S. editions from 2004 to 2009, deals with a curse that turns members of a prominent family into animals of the Chinese zodiac. The cursed characters are human most of the time, but often view themselves as monsters.

- Joseph D. Andrioano's *Immortal Monster* (1999) discusses *The Island of Dr. Moreau* in connection with its film adaptations and in the genre of fictional monsters.

- Part of the power of the concept of *The Island of Dr. Moreau* comes from its updated treatment of the boundary that exists between animal and human. This idea is a prominent feature of world mythology in the concept of half-human, half-animal creatures, such as a faun, and of beings such as werewolves that can change between the two states. Rosemary Guiley's 2004 *The Encyclopedia of Vampires, Werewolves, and Other Monsters*, published for young adults, surveys world mythology and folklore for such monstrous crossovers of the human-animal boundary.

- Edwin Black's popular 2004 history of the eugenics movement, *War against the Weak: Eugenics and America's Campaign to Create a Master Race*, shows how the eugenics movement and the Holocaust arose from pseudo-scientific misunderstandings of biological science.

- Of Wells's own works, his 1895 novel, *The Time Machine*, most closely approaches *The Island of Dr. Moreau*'s theme of human degeneration.

Sources

Aldiss, Brian, and David Wingrove, *Trillion Year Spree: The History of Science Fiction*, V. Gollancz, 1986.

Freud, Sigmund, *The Future of an Illusion*, translated by James Strachey, W. W. Norton, 1961.

Galton, Francis, "Eugenics: Its Definition, Scope, and Aims," in *American Journal of Sociology*, Vol. 10, July/May 1904–1905, pp. 10–11.

Guerrini, Anita, *Experimenting with Humans and Animals from Galen to Animal Rights*, Johns Hopkins University Press, 2003.

Holzberg, Niklas, *The Ancient Novel: An Introduction*, translated by Christine Jackson-Hollzberg, Routledge, 1995.

Huxley, Thomas H., *Evolution and Ethics and Other Essays*, D. Appleton, 1920, pp. 1–45, http://books.google.   com/books?id=CbzZAAAAMAAJ&source=gbs_navlinks_s (accessed June 30, 2010).

Kemp, Peter, *H. G. Wells and the Culminating Ape: Biological Imperatives and Imaginative Observations*, Macmillan, 1992, pp. 19–23, 201–203.

McLean, Steven, *The Early Fictions of H. G. Wells: Fantasies of Science*, Palgrave MacMillan, 2009, pp. 41–61.

Parrinder, Patrick, ed., *H. G. Wells: The Critical Heritage*, Routledge and Kegan Paul, 1972, pp. 43–56, 330–32.

Reed, John R., "The Vanity of Law in *The Island of Dr. Moreau*," in *H. G. Wells under Revision: Proceedings of the International H. G. Wells Symposium, London, 1986*, edited by Patrick Parrinder and Christopher Rolfe, Susquehanna University Press, 1990, pp. 132–43.

Rupke, Nicolaas, A., *Vivisection in Historical Perspective*, Welcome Institute, 1990.

Smith, David C., *H. G. Wells: Desperately Mortal, A Biography*, Yale University Press, 1986.

Stover, Leon, "Applied Natural History: Wells vs. Huxley," in *H. G. Wells under Revision: Proceedings of the International H. G. Wells Symposium, London, 1986*, edited by Patrick Parrinder and Christopher Rolfe, Susquehanna University Press, 1990, pp. 125–33.

Swift, Jonathan, *Gulliver's Travels*, Oxford University Press, 1919.

Wells, H. G., *Experiment in Autobiography: Discoveries and Conclusions of a Very Ordinary Brain (Since 1866)*, MacMillan, 1934.

Wells, H. G., *The Island of Doctor Moreau: A Variorum Text*, edited by Robert M. Philmus, University of Georgia Press, 1993.

Wells, H. G., *The Island of Dr. Moreau: A Critical Text of the 1896 London First Edition, with an Introduction and Appendices*, edited by Leon

Stover, McFarlane, 1996.

Wells, H. G., *Works, Vol II: The Island of Dr. Moreau, The Sleeper Wakes*, Charles Scribner, 1924.

Williamson, Jack, *H. G. Wells: Critic of Progress*, Mirage, 1973, pp. 74–82.

Further Reading

Draper, Michael, *Modern Novelists: H. G. Wells*, St. Martin's Press, 1988.

> Draper provides a biographical and literary survey of Wells's work.

Hammond, J. R., *H. G. Wells: Interviews and Recollections*, Barnes & Noble, 1980.

> Hammond collects press interviews and brief autobiographical published articles with or by Wells.

Kevles, Daniel J., *In the Name of Eugenics: Genetics and the Uses of Human Heredity*, Harvard University Press, 1995.

> Kevles chronicles the standard history of the eugenics movement.

Suvin, Darko, and Robert M. Philmus, eds., *H. G. Wells and Modern Science Fiction*, Bucknell University Press, 1977.

> This anthology contains scholarly articles analyzing Wells from a variety of perspectives. Several touch on *The Island of Dr. Moreau* in relation to traditional folklore and fantasy literature, rather than science fiction.